WHOLE FOODS DIET FOR WELLNESS

A Journey to Vibrant Life

ROLL ALEX

TABLE OF CONTENTS

01 | Introduction to Whole Foods
The Philosophy of Whole Foods
Benefits of Whole Foods for Health
Understanding Processed vs. Whole Foods

02 | The Science Behind Whole Foods
Nutritional Components of Whole Foods
Impact on Chronic Diseases
The Gut-Brain Connection

03 | Getting Started with Whole Foods
Assessing Your Current Diet
Setting Realistic Goals
Kitchen Essentials for Whole Foods

04 | Meal Planning and Preparation
Creating a Whole Foods Meal Plan
Batch Cooking and Meal Prep Strategies
Grocery Shopping Tips for Whole Foods

05 | Whole Foods Cooking Techniques
Cooking Methods for Nutrient Preservation
Flavoring with Herbs and Spices
Quick and Easy Whole Foods Recipes

TABLE OF CONTENTS

06 | **Navigating Dietary Restrictions**
Whole Foods for Various Diets
(Vegan, Gluten-Free, etc.)
Managing Food Allergies
Balancing Nutritional Needs

07 | **Whole Foods and Mental Wellness**
The Role of Nutrition in Mental Health
Foods that Boost Mood and Focus
Mindful Eating Practices

08 | **Whole Foods for Families**
Introducing Whole Foods to Children
Family Meal Ideas
Encouraging Healthy Eating Habits

09 | **Overcoming Challenges**
Common Obstacles and Solutions
Staying Motivated on Your Journey
Building a Support Network

10 | **: Celebrating Your Progress**
Reflecting on Your Journey
Sharing Your Experience with Others
Continuing the Whole Foods Lifestyle

INTRODUCTION TO WHOLE FOODS

THE PHILOSOPHY OF WHOLE FOODS

Consuming food in its most natural state, as near to its original form as possible, is central to the whole foods philosophy. This method highlights the value of complete, unadulterated foods that are nutrient-dense and devoid of artificial additives. Individuals can improve their general health and well-being by giving priority to certain foods. This ideology is based on the idea that our physical, mental, and emotional well-being are significantly influenced by the foods we eat.

The idea of nourishment is central to the whole foods philosophy. Essential vitamins, minerals, and antioxidants are found in whole foods such fruits, vegetables, whole grains, nuts, and seeds. Whole foods assist the body's natural processes and aid in healing, in contrast to processed and refined foods, which frequently lack nutritional value. This method teaches people to see food as a source of energy and vitality that may support a vibrant life, rather than just as a means of obtaining nourishment.

Sustainability is another important component of this concept. The trend toward whole foods frequently coincides with actions that promote environmental health, such selecting seasonal and locally grown produce. People may help create a more sustainable food system that lowers the carbon footprint of food production and transportation by choosing whole foods. This link between environmental stewardship and personal health highlights how important it is to make thoughtful dietary choices that benefit both the environment and the individual.

INTRODUCTION TO WHOLE FOODS

THE PHILOSOPHY OF WHOLE FOODS

A stronger bond with food and preparation is also promoted by the whole foods philosophy. As participants are encouraged to try out novel products and cooking techniques, culinary exploration becomes an essential component of this adventure. Eating is made more interesting and enjoyable by this hands-on approach, which cultivates a deeper appreciation for the tastes and textures of complete foods. People can develop a more conscious relationship with their meals by enjoying the creativity that goes into making complete foods.

In the end, the whole foods philosophy promotes a comprehensive strategy for wellbeing and health. It encourages people to take care of themselves on many levels by acknowledging the connection between the body, mind, and spirit. Health enthusiasts, those with chronic illnesses, nutrition and wellness specialists, and food adventurers can all experience a life-changing journey that fosters not just physical health but also emotional fortitude and spiritual fulfillment by embracing a whole foods diet. This concept, which is based on the ideas of mindful living and natural nourishment, can help people live more balanced and energetic lives.

Benefits of Whole Foods for Health

There are several health advantages to eating whole foods, which are crucial for preserving good health. Whole foods are high in vital nutrients since they are barely processed and devoid of artificial additives. Fruits, vegetables, whole grains, legumes, nuts, and seeds are some examples of these foods. People can greatly increase their intake of vitamins, minerals, and fiber—all of which are essential for body functions—by concentrating on whole foods. This nutrient density boosts energy levels, supports immunological function, and helps prevent chronic illnesses.

The capacity of a whole foods diet to aid with weight management is among its most important benefits. While still offering the nutrients the body need, whole foods frequently have fewer calories than their processed counterparts. Fruits, vegetables, and whole grains are rich in fiber, which can increase feelings of fullness and perhaps lower total caloric consumption. Without using restrictive diets, people can more easily maintain a healthy weight or reach their weight loss objectives because to this satiety effect.

Lastly, following a whole foods diet promotes a more mindful and sustainable way of eating. Because they take less resources to produce and package, whole foods generally have a smaller environmental effect than processed foods. This feature has a good impact on the environment in addition to improving individual health. Choosing whole foods is something that health enthusiasts, dietitians, and food adventurers can all be proud of since it creates a stronger bond with the food system and encourages a way of life that prioritizes sustainability, health, and the welfare of the community.

Comprehending Whole vs. Processed Foods

Additionally, eating healthy meals can improve mental wellness. Recent studies indicate a robust relationship between mental health and nutrition. Whole foods high in nutrients can boost cognitive function, lower anxiety, and improve mood. Brain health can be supported by foods strong in omega-3 fatty acids, like walnuts and flaxseeds, and foods high in B vitamins, including leafy greens and legumes. Making whole foods a priority may help people feel more balanced emotionally and think more clearly.

There are several stages into which processed foods can be divided. Some, like frozen fruits and vegetables, are little processed and nonetheless have a high nutritional content. Others, including sugary cereals, quick food, and prepared meals, experience major changes that frequently deprive them of vital nutrients. In addition to changing the food's natural form, this intensive processing raises the food's caloric density while lowering its nutritional value. Knowing these categories is essential for helping nutritionists and health enthusiasts make better food selections as they navigate dietary requirements.

It is impossible to overestimate the health effects of eating processed foods as opposed to whole foods. Diets rich in whole foods are consistently linked to decreased incidence of chronic illnesses, such as diabetes, heart disease, and several types of cancer, according to research. Whole foods are good for controlling weight because they increase feelings of fullness and help control blood sugar levels. Conversely, diets heavy in processed foods can exacerbate metabolic syndrome, obesity, and inflammation. People who prioritize whole foods develop a more lively lifestyle in addition to improving their physical health.

CHAPTER 2
THE SCIENCE BEHIND WHOLE FOODS

Nutritional Components of Whole Foods

Unprocessed or lightly processed foods that preserve their inherent nutrients and qualities are referred to as whole foods. Fruits, vegetables, whole grains, legumes, nuts, seeds, and animal products devoid of artificial additives are examples of these foods. Whole foods have a variety of nutritious components that greatly improve general health. They offer fiber, good fats, antioxidants, and vital vitamins and minerals—all of which are vital for maintaining healthy body functions and preventing disease.

Vitamins and minerals, which are abundant in fruits and vegetables, are essential for sustaining a number of body processes. For example, potassium in leafy greens helps control blood pressure, and vitamin C in citrus foods boosts the immune system. Antioxidants like flavonoids and carotenoids, which fight inflammation and oxidative stress, are also abundant in these plant-based diets. Because of their preventive properties, which can lower the risk of chronic illnesses like cancer and heart disease, fruits and vegetables are essential parts of a whole foods diet.

Another crucial dietary element is whole grains, such quinoa, brown rice, and oats. They are great providers of complex carbs, which give you energy for a long time without making your blood sugar jump. Significant levels of dietary fiber, which facilitates digestion and supports a balanced gut microbiota, are also found in whole grains. Fiber promotes satiety and lowers cholesterol, which makes it simpler to keep a healthy weight. Long-term health can be improved and nutrient intake increased by including a range of whole grains in the diet.

Nuts and seeds are superfoods that are high in protein, good fats, and other nutrients. Omega-3 and omega-6 fatty acids, which are vital for brain function and inflammation reduction, are abundant in them. Minerals including magnesium, zinc, and selenium, which are essential for immunological and metabolic functions, are also found in nuts and seeds. Nutrient density can be greatly increased and general wellness can be enhanced by adding a handful of nuts or a sprinkle of seeds to daily meals.

Last but not least, whole food animal products provide high-quality protein and necessary fatty acids. Examples of these are eggs, wild-caught fish, and grass-fed meats. Complete proteins with all nine essential amino acids required for muscle growth and repair are found in these foods. Vitamins like B12, which are essential for neurological and energy metabolism, are also abundant in them

10

Selecting animal products from sustainable sources can promote ethical and environmental concerns while improving a whole foods diet. In addition to promoting healthy health, highlighting the nutritional components of entire foods also helps us develop a stronger bond with the food we eat.

Effects on Long-Term Conditions

Whole foods have a significant and diverse influence on chronic illnesses, providing a comprehensive approach to health that goes beyond simple dietary adjustments. Chronic conditions including diabetes, heart disease, and obesity are frequently associated with lifestyle choices, inflammation, and dietary deficiencies. People can greatly lower their chances of getting these illnesses and enhance their general quality of life by including whole foods in their daily meals. Whole foods—those that are minimally processed and free of artificial ingredients—offer vital nutrients that support physiological processes and aid in the healing process.

Diets high in whole foods have been repeatedly demonstrated to reduce the prevalence of chronic illnesses. Vitamins, minerals, antioxidants, and dietary fiber, for example, are abundant in fruits, vegetables, whole grains, nuts, and seeds. These nutrients are essential for controlling blood sugar, lowering inflammation, and promoting cardiovascular health. While a diet rich in fiber and heart-healthy fats can help those at risk of heart disease, a whole foods diet can help people with diabetes stabilize their blood sugar levels and lessen their need for medication.

It is impossible to overestimate the importance of whole foods in the fight against obesity. Because processed meals are frequently high in calories and low in nutrients, they can cause overeating and weight gain. On the other hand, because of their high fiber content, whole foods have a satiating effect that encourages feelings of fullness and lowers the risk of overeating. Whole foods also aid in metabolic regulation, which is critical for preserving a healthy weight. The opportunity to experiment with a variety of whole food products that not only support the body but also foster culinary creativity is presented to health enthusiasts and culinary adventurers.

In order to effectively guide clients with chronic health conditions, wellness practitioners must have a solid understanding of the nutritional science underlying whole foods. People can be empowered to make wise decisions by being informed about the advantages of including more whole foods in their diets. Because whole foods can offer natural strategies to lower blood pressure and enhance lipid profiles without the adverse effects frequently associated with medicines, this information can be especially helpful for those managing diseases like hypertension or high cholesterol.

In conclusion, the ability of nutrition to support health and wellness is demonstrated by the effect of whole foods on chronic illnesses. People can promote a lifestyle that not only minimizes chronic diseases but also improves general vitality by emphasizing complete, unprocessed foods. This method stresses the value of food quality above quantity and promotes a change from short-term diets to long-term eating patterns. Adopting whole foods can result in a life-changing path toward vibrant health for nutrition experts, chronic condition sufferers, and health enthusiasts alike.

The Link Between the Gut and the Brain

A intriguing field of research that emphasizes the complex interplay between the brain and the gastrointestinal system is the gut-brain connection. A complex web of channels, including hormones, neurotransmitters, and the vagus nerve, underlies this link. A key player in this conversation is the gut microbiome, which is made up of the billions of bacteria that live in our intestines. It affects emotions, thought processes, and general mental health in addition to digestion and food absorption. Knowing this relationship can help nutritionists and health enthusiasts make dietary decisions that support gut and brain health.

Studies have demonstrated that the gut microbiota can generate neurotransmitters like serotonin, sometimes known as the "feel-good" hormone. The gut produces over 90% of the serotonin in the body. According to this link, our mental health can be directly impacted by the things we eat. Whole foods high in nutrients and fiber can promote a varied microbiome, which enhances mood and cognitive performance. Foods that promote the growth of good bacteria, such as whole grains, legumes, and fermented vegetables, help improve the gut-brain link.

On the other hand, a diet heavy in processed foods, sweets, and bad fats can upset the microbiota and cause mood disorders including depression and anxiety. A vicious loop can result from the inflammation brought on by bad food choices, which can drive the brain to react negatively. Understanding how diet affects gut health and mental state is especially beneficial for people with chronic diseases. They can reduce inflammation and encourage a better gut environment by emphasizing whole meals, which may enhance emotional stability and mental clarity.

By experimenting with different whole food items that support both systems, culinary explorers can also take advantage of the gut-brain connection. Nuts, seeds, omega-3-rich fatty fish, and a range of vibrant fruits and vegetables can all be included to supply vital nutrients that promote brain function. Probiotics can also be added to food using culinary methods like fermentation, which can improve gut health even more. In addition to enhancing the palate, this investigation gives people the confidence to take control of their health by practicing mindful eating.

To sum up, the gut-brain connection emphasizes how crucial nutrition is to attaining flourishing health. Embracing the whole foods diet can open the door to better mental and physical well-being for health enthusiasts, nutrition and wellness specialists, and culinary adventurers alike. People can create a healthy, more vibrant existence by giving priority to foods that promote the microbiota and lower inflammation. This will create a harmonic interaction between the gut and the brain.

Chapter 3

Getting Started with Whole Foods

Assessing Your Current Diet

One of the most important steps in making the switch to a whole foods lifestyle is evaluating your current diet. This method entails examining your daily diet in detail, assessing the nutritional value of your meals, and pinpointing areas that require improvement. Start by maintaining a thorough food journal for a minimum of one week. Keep track of everything you eat and drink, including snacks and supplements. This will provide you a clear picture of your eating patterns and enable you to identify the foods that make up the majority of your diet.

Sort the entries in your food journal into two categories: whole foods and processed foods. Whole foods are minimally processed and devoid of artificial substances, such as fruits, vegetables, whole grains, nuts, seeds, and lean proteins. On the other hand, processed foods frequently have high levels of sugar or salt, preservatives, and additives. You can determine how closely you adhere to the tenets of a whole foods diet by visually evaluating the percentage of whole foods in your diet. To maximize your nutritious intake, try to achieve a greater proportion of whole foods to processed meals.

Next, assess how well your meals balance the macronutrients. A balanced diet should include the right proportions of lipids, proteins, and carbs. Numerous nutrients included in whole foods support general health. For instance, your body is fueled by complex carbs found in whole grains and veggies, while your brain is supported by healthy fats found in avocados and nuts. In addition to macronutrients, take note of micronutrients—vitamins and minerals that are necessary for numerous biological processes. If your diet is significantly biased toward one macronutrient, think about modifying it to attain a more balanced intake that supports your body's needs. These nutrients are abundant in whole foods, but with a diet high in processed foods, it's simple to forget about them. To find any possible nutritional intake gaps, go over your meal journal. Do you consume enough fruits and veggies each day? In order to guarantee a broad range of vitamins and minerals, are you eating a diversity of colors? Including a variety of whole foods in your meals will help you properly achieve your micronutrient requirements.

Lastly, consider your general lifestyle and eating patterns. Think about things like meal scheduling, portion amounts, and how mindfully you consume. Do you eat because you're hungry or just out of habit? Do you frequently eat your meals quickly or do you take the time to enjoy them? Eating mindfully can improve your relationship with food and increase your awareness of your body's cues. You can develop a more comprehensive approach to your diet that is in line with the ideas of vibrant health by evaluating both what and how you eat.

Establishing Reasonable Objectives

One of the most important steps to successfully implementing a whole foods diet over the long run is setting reasonable goals. Many people go out on this road with grand goals, like losing weight quickly or significantly altering their eating habits overnight. However, when results do not appear as soon as expected, these goals can frequently result in irritation and disappointment. Throughout their path to vibrant health, people can sustain motivation and cultivate a sense of success by setting small, attainable goals.

Assessing your present eating patterns and way of life is crucial first. You can pinpoint particular areas for development by using this self-evaluation tool. For example, adding a specific amount of whole foods to your meals each week could be a feasible goal if your present diet is highly processed. Focus on progressively replacing processed foods with whole food alternatives rather than trying to completely eradicate them all at once. The adjustment period may be shortened and the move may seem less daunting with this gradual transition

Setting quantifiable objectives that can be monitored over time is also crucial. Instead of announcing a general goal to "eat healthier," think about defining concrete steps, such deciding to prepare three meals a week at home with whole ingredients. In addition to providing a clear road map, quantifying your goals also makes it possible for you to recognize and appreciate minor accomplishments along the way. In addition to boosting confidence in your capacity to maintain these changes, this technique encourages beneficial behavior.

Making sure your goals fit your lifestyle and personal values is another crucial component of creating realistic goals. Different priorities and situations may affect the food choices of wellness professionals, chronic illness sufferers, and health enthusiasts. As such, tailoring your objectives to your particular circumstances is essential. Setting a goal to prepare meals ahead of time, for instance, can help you stick to your whole foods commitment without feeling rushed or deprived if you have a hectic schedule.

Finally, it's critical to maintain your flexibility and be willing to change your objectives as necessary. Because life is unpredictable, a number of things, including stress, travel, or health problems, may affect your ability to stick to your plan. You can reevaluate and adjust your goals without feeling defeated if you have an adaptable mindset. Keep in mind that achieving robust health is a lifelong process of learning and development rather than a race. You can develop a fulfilling and long-lasting connection with healthy foods that improves your general well-being by establishing attainable, customized goals.

Essential Kitchenware for Whole Foods

Having the proper kitchen tools is key for a seamless and pleasurable cooking experience when starting a whole foods diet. These necessities promote a lifestyle focused on whole, unadulterated foods while also making it easier to prepare wholesome meals. Purchasing top-notch tools and equipment can turn your kitchen into a useful area that fosters creativity and well-being.

Above all, a quality set of knives is essential. You may easily prepare fresh fruits, veggies, and whole grains with a chef's knife, paring knife, and serrated knife, which will handle the majority of your cutting needs. Furthermore, a solid cutting board composed of oak or bamboo will offer a dependable surface that safeguards your knives and promotes food safety. Your knives will continue to be safe and effective for cutting if you do routine maintenance, such as honing and sharpening them.

Another crucial component of a whole foods kitchen is cookware. Choose cast iron or stainless steel pots and pans since they are long-lasting and don't contain the dangerous chemicals present in non-stick coatings. For making smoothies, soups, and sauces that include whole ingredients, a good blender is also essential. For more intricate preparations that can greatly improve the flavors and textures of your meals, such dips, nut butters, and finely chopped veggies, think about including a food processor.

Storage containers are essential for preparing meals and preserving ingredients. To preserve freshness and minimize food waste, prepped vegetables, grains, and leftovers are best stored in glass containers with airtight covers. By labeling these containers, you can maintain kitchen organization and facilitate ingredient access throughout meal preparation. Moreover, using reusable produce bags can promote bulk purchasing, enabling you to get fresh, whole meals while reducing plastic waste.

Lastly, a healthy whole foods diet depends on having a range of pantry essentials available. Keep legumes like chickpeas and lentils on hand, along with nutritious grains like quinoa, brown rice, and oats. In addition to adding texture to meals, a variety of nuts, seeds, and dried fruits can make nutritious snacks. Herbs and spices are also essential for boosting flavor without adding unhealthy components or extra sodium. You may assist your journey to robust health by using these kitchen necessities to prepare tasty, healthy meals that adhere to the whole foods diet's tenets

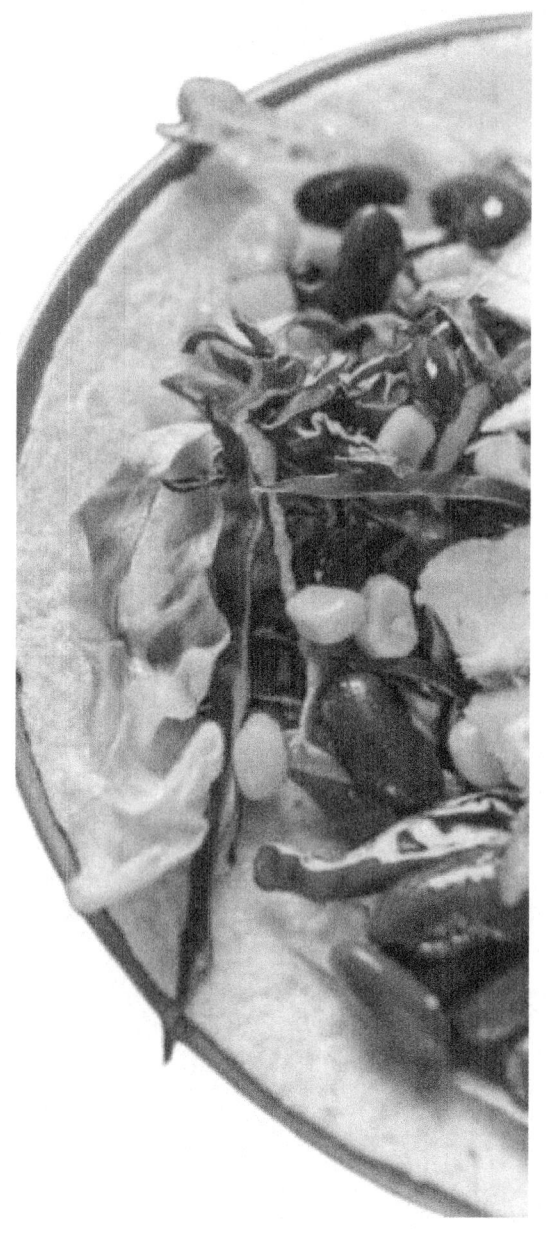

Chapter 4

MEAL PLANNING AND PREPARATION

Creating a Whole Foods Meal Plan

Choosing and cooking meals that support general health and nourish the body requires careful consideration when creating a whole foods meal plan. Consuming minimally processed foods that are as close to their original state as possible forms the basis of a whole foods diet. This entails eschewing processed sugars, refined oils, and artificial additives in favor of fresh fruits, vegetables, whole grains, legumes, nuts, and seeds. Understanding the fundamentals of whole foods and how to successfully and sustainably include them into regular meals is crucial when starting this path.

Assessing your dietary requirements and preferences is the first step in creating a meal plan. Take into account any allergies, intolerances, or medical issues that can affect the foods you choose. Consider your timetable and way of life as well. Do you have time to try out new recipes or do you require quick meals for hectic days? In order to make sure you are getting all the nutrients you need, you may use this information to develop a balanced meal plan that consists of a range of foods. Because different colors of produce frequently imply distinct nutrient profiles, try to include a rainbow of vegetables in your meals.

It's time to organize your meal plan after you've compiled a list of your favorite foods. Three major meals and two to three snacks each day could be part of a usual schedule. A smoothie full of protein and leafy greens or oatmeal with fresh fruit and almonds on top are good choices for breakfast. A substantial salad with a range of vibrant veggies, cereals, and a protein source like grilled chicken or chickpeas may make up lunch. Quinoa, roasted veggies, and a healthy fat like avocado or olive oil can all be included in a warm dinner. A piece of fruit, a handful of nuts, or raw vegetables with hummus can all serve as snacks to keep you going all day.

Purchasing whole foods is essential to your meal plan's success. Start by creating a shopping list based on the meals you intend to eat, paying particular attention to the area of the supermarket where fresh vegetables, meats, and dairy goods are usually located. Bulk purchases can also be an affordable option to stock up on nuts, legumes, and grains. Read labels carefully when purchasing packaged goods to steer clear of additives and hidden sugars. Making meal preparation a weekly routine might help you save time and concentrate on enjoying your meals rather than rushing to pull something together at the last minute.

Lastly, keep in mind that a whole foods meal plan is dynamic and should change according to your body's input, seasonal availability, and personal tastes. To keep your meals interesting and captivating, try out different recipes and components. You can improve your overall experience and enjoyment by using mindful eating techniques, such as enjoying every bite and paying attention to your body's hunger cues. You may create a nourishing and energetic lifestyle that promotes your health and well-being by adopting the tenets of a whole foods diet and preparing your meals with intention.

Strategies for Meal Preparation and Batch Cooking

Anybody following a whole foods diet has to know how to prepare meals and cook in bulk. Making meals ahead of time helps people avoid the temptation of processed foods by ensuring they always have wholesome, nutrient-dense options on hand. This technique encourages thoughtful eating habits in addition to saving time during the hectic week. Maintaining a balanced diet is made simpler when meals are prepared in bulk since people can choose the type and quality of the foods they eat.

First, creating a weekly food plan is the first step in batch cooking. This entails choosing dishes that highlight a variety of vegetables, whole grains, legumes, and lean proteins, as well as seasonal whole foods. Making a shopping list based on these recipes makes grocery shopping more efficient and guarantees that all required materials are available. People can improve their nutritional intake and help achieve their overall health goals by giving whole foods priority.

Setting aside a certain day to prepare meals after shopping is finished is essential. For many people, cooking in greater quantities is best done on the weekends. People can wash, cut, and prepare items during this period, which speeds up the cooking process. In addition to saving time, bulk cooking of grains, roasting of vegetables, and preparation of proteins like chicken or tofu enables a variety of meals to be prepared throughout the week. It is simpler to mix and match ingredients for various meals when these components are kept in clear containers.

Using freezer-friendly dinnerware is another smart tactic. The best foods to freeze are soups, stews, and casseroles since they keep their flavor and nutritional content well. These meals are great for quick lunches or dinners because they are portioned into individual servings. It can also be advantageous to include snacks in the meal preparation process. Making foods like whole grain muffins, energy balls, or chopped fruits and veggies in advance guarantees that there are always wholesome options available, which lowers the chance of opting for less nourishing snacks.

Lastly, the secret to long-term success in batch cooking is to embrace flexibility. While preparation is crucial, cooking creativity can be increased by being willing to modify recipes in response to what is in season or accessible. Meals may remain interesting and pleasurable by experimenting with various spices, herbs, and cooking techniques. People may develop a sustainable whole foods lifestyle and make it simpler to fuel their bodies and embrace robust health by implementing these batch cooking and meal prep techniques

Whole Foods Grocery Shopping Tips

It's crucial to have a well-defined plan before starting a whole foods grocery shopping excursion. Plan your meals for the coming week beforehand. This assists you in making a targeted shopping list that reduces impulsive buys and guarantees you have everything you need to make wholesome meals. Spend some time looking at recipes that use whole grains, lean meats, healthy fats, and seasonal produce. In addition to saving time, a well-organized itinerary promotes a more pleasurable and thoughtful shopping experience.

Choosing the best whole foods requires knowing how to properly navigate the grocery market. There are plenty of fresh fruits and vegetables in the produce department, so start your shopping there. To optimize nutritional intake and guarantee a varied diet, try to find a range of colors and varieties. Selecting organic products whenever feasible can help promote sustainable farming methods and lessen pesticide exposure. Additionally, don't be afraid to ask employees for advice or pointers on how to choose the freshest products. In addition to improving your shopping experience, this may help you find new ingredients that you may incorporate into your diet on a regular basis.

Understanding labels and ingredients is a crucial part of supermarket shopping for whole foods. Learn the difference between whole foods and those that are advertised as healthy yet contain preservatives or additives. Choose products with short ingredient lists and little processing, emphasizing whole grains, legumes, nuts, seeds, and unprocessed oils. Gaining the ability to critically read labels will enable you to make decisions that are in line with your dietary preferences and health objectives.

Consider purchasing at your neighborhood co-op or farmers' market, which can provide a larger assortment of whole food items and fresh, in-season produce. In addition to helping your community, supporting local agriculture guarantees that the food you eat is frequently harvested at its ripest, which improves its flavor and nutritional content. Developing ties with nearby farmers can also help you learn about seasonal cuisine and even cooking techniques that will further your culinary adventure.

Lastly, keep in mind that buying whole foods at the grocery store may be enjoyable and fulfilling. Make it a social gathering where you may exchange inspiration and ideas by involving your loved ones. Don't be scared to explore new cuisines and try different ingredients. This method enhances your meals and fosters a greater understanding of the range of whole foods that are accessible. Including these grocery shopping suggestions into your daily routine can help you develop a healthy, active lifestyle that will help you reach your full potential.

CHAPTER 5
Whole Foods Cooking Techniques

Cooking Methods for Nutrient Preservation

Cooking techniques are essential for preserving nutrients, particularly for people who eat a whole foods diet. Selecting cooking methods that preserve the integrity of whole foods is crucial because they are little processed and retain their natural nutrients. The nutritional value of fruits, vegetables, grains, and proteins can be greatly impacted by a variety of techniques. Health enthusiasts, people with chronic illnesses, nutritionists, wellness specialists, and food adventurers can all make well-informed culinary decisions that promote optimal health by being aware of these techniques.

One of the best cooking techniques for maintaining nutrients is steaming. Instead of immersing food in water, which can cause vitamins and minerals to leach, this method cooks food in steam. Important elements, especially water-soluble vitamins like C and B vitamins, are retained during steaming. Avoiding overcooking is essential for successful steaming because extended heat exposure can still impair nutritional levels. Cooks can guarantee that their food is not only tasty but also nutrient-dense by choosing steaming over boiling or frying.

Sautéing, which entails rapidly cooking food in a minimal quantity of healthful fat, is another advantageous technique. Vegetables benefit well from this method since it preserves their bright colors and crunchy textures. Additionally, sautéing helps fat-soluble vitamins like A, D, E, and K be better absorbed. Lower heat and shorter cooking times are recommended to maximize nutrient retention because they stop sensitive nutrients from breaking down. The health advantages of this cooking technique are further increased by using premium oils, such as avocado or olive oil.

Roasting is a common technique that enhances the flavor of whole foods while preserving nutrients. Roasting vegetables and proteins causes them to caramelize, which intensifies their inherent sweetness and produces a pleasing texture. Roasting can efficiently preserve nutrients even though it involves greater temperatures, particularly when food is cooked whole or in larger pieces. It is crucial to keep an eye on cooking temperatures and periods to prevent excessive char or burning, which can produce toxic chemicals, in order to preserve nutrient density.

Last but not least, adding raw food preparation to the diet can significantly increase nutritional intake. Since cooking can damage heat-sensitive vitamins and enzymes, many fruits and vegetables are more nutrient-dense when consumed raw. These foods can be enjoyed in their most nutrient-dense form in salads, smoothies, and fresh juices. To guarantee a varied nutrient intake, it is crucial to balance the consumption of raw and cooked foods. Furthermore, cooking some foods—like tomatoes and carrots—actually increases their accessible nutrients, highlighting the necessity of a diverse approach to food preparation.

In conclusion, everybody on a whole foods diet has to understand how to cook in order to preserve nutrients. People can maximize the nutritional value of their meals by selecting methods such as roasting, sautéing, steaming, and adding raw preparations. This information improves the whole culinary experience while also assisting with personal health objectives. Mindful cooking techniques that honor the integrity of whole foods are the first step towards robust health for health enthusiasts, people with chronic diseases, nutrition and wellness specialists, and culinary adventurers.

Using Spices and Herbs to Flavor

A vital component of the whole foods diet, flavoring using herbs and spices not only improves the taste of food but also has many health advantages. Plants are the source of herbs and spices, which are abundant in bioactive substances such as antioxidants and essential oils. By adding these natural flavor enhancers to your diet, you can increase your immune system, reduce inflammation, and improve digestion, among other health consequences. You can improve your cooking while adhering to the whole foods philosophy by using herbs and spices instead of artificial flavorings.

Vibrant flavors and vital minerals are provided by fresh herbs including parsley, cilantro, and basil. Vitamins A, C, and K, which support general health and wellbeing, are especially abundant in them. Fresh herbs are simple to add into regular cooking and may be used in a wide range of recipes, including soups and salads. They are also affordable and accessible for both health-conscious people and food adventurers because they can be cultivated in tiny pots at home. In addition to adding flavor, the freshness of homegrown herbs fosters a closer bond with the food you eat.

Whole foods can benefit greatly from the seasoning of dried herbs and spices, such as oregano, thyme, cinnamon, and turmeric. These ingredients provide depth and complexity to a variety of cuisines and are easily preserved. Turmeric and other spices have drawn interest due to their anti-inflammatory qualities and possible health advantages, which include promoting joint health and enhancing digestion. People can find distinctive flavor profiles that make eating healthily pleasurable and fulfilling by experimenting with various mixes of dried herbs and spices.

The way herbs and spices are prepared can have a big impact on their flavor and health benefits. Toasting spices before using them is one method that releases essential oils and improves their flavor and scent. Dried oregano can be introduced early to develop its flavor, while fresh basil can be added at the end of cooking to preserve its bright taste. Similarly, adding herbs at different stages of cooking might result in distinct flavors. Culinary adventurers can optimize the effects of herbs and spices in their dishes by being aware of these methods.

In the end, adding flavor with herbs and spices is an essential part of a holistic approach to health, not just a way to improve taste. You can experience a variety of flavors and benefit from the numerous health advantages that these natural substances provide by include a wide range of them in your diet. Promoting the use of herbs and spices can be a potent strategy for nutritionists and health enthusiasts to inspire people to embrace whole foods and develop a greater understanding of the relationship between food, health, and vibrant life.

SIMPLE AND FAST RECIPES FOR WHOLE FOODS

It's not difficult or time-consuming to include whole foods in your regular meals. You may adopt a whole foods diet without compromising taste or nutrients by following simple and quick recipes. The secret is to concentrate on basic, minimally processed products so that you can make wholesome and fulfilling meals. In order to make it simpler for health enthusiasts, those with long-term illnesses, and food adventurers to savor colorful, healthful meals, this subchapter will offer a range of recipes that showcase the beauty of whole foods.

A great place to start is with a satisfying and refreshing quinoa salad. Start by preparing one cup of quinoa per the directions on the package. After cooking, let it cool and then add a variety of vibrant veggies, like chopped cucumbers, cherry tomatoes, and diced bell peppers. Add some fresh herbs, such as cilantro or parsley, for taste, then garnish the salad with a drizzle of olive oil and a squeeze of lemon juice. In just a few minutes, this recipe highlights the rich aromas of healthy foods while also being a wonderful source of fiber and protein.

A stir-fry with lean protein and seasonal vegetables is another easy choice. Pick some of your favorite veggies, such carrots, snap peas, and broccoli. Quickly sauté the vegetables in a pan with a tablespoon of heated coconut oil until they are crisp-tender. For protein, add sliced chicken breast or tofu. For flavor depth, add garlic and low-sodium soy sauce. Serve on top of brown rice or cauliflower rice for a filling, healthy, and incredibly fulfilling supper.

Overnight oats are a great whole foods option for anyone seeking a substantial meal that only takes a few minutes to make the night before. Add chia seeds, nuts, and fresh or frozen fruit as garnishes after mixing the rolled oats with your preferred milk or yogurt. To give the oats time to absorb the liquid and become softer, leave the mixture in the fridge overnight. You have a tasty and nourishing breakfast ready to eat in the morning, full of fiber and vital nutrients to start the day off well.

Last but not least, a straightforward yet delicious smoothie that is full of whole food deliciousness can be used as a quick supper or snack. Put a cup of unsweetened almond milk, a handful of spinach, a spoonful of almond butter, and a ripe banana in a blender. For an extra nutritional boost, feel free to add ingredients like protein powder or flax seeds after blending until smooth. In addition to being simple to make, this smoothie is a fantastic way to include greens and healthy fats to your diet, which promotes general health and vitality.

Healthy meals may easily fit into a hectic lifestyle, as these quick and simple whole foods recipes show. You can savor delectable flavors and stick to your whole foods diet by concentrating on simple, whole components. These recipes are meant to encourage and empower you on your path to vibrant health, regardless of whether you are a health enthusiast, someone managing a chronic illness, or a foodie looking to try new flavors

Chapter 6
Navigating Dietary Restrictions

Whole Foods for Various Diets (Vegan, Gluten-Free, etc.)

The foundation of many dietary regimens is made up of whole foods, which minimize processed components while offering vital nutrients. Whole foods include many different types of fruits, vegetables, legumes, nuts, and seeds for vegans. This plant-based strategy prioritizes fresh, unprocessed foods while avoiding animal products. Vegan diets can take many forms, including colorful salads, filling grain bowls, and creative plant-based alternatives that don't lose flavor or texture. People may make sure they're getting enough protein, good fats, and a variety of vitamins and minerals by emphasizing whole foods, which also supports sustainable farming methods.

Whole foods offer a wealth of options that inherently omit gluten-containing grains for people following a gluten-free diet. Wholesome substitutes that are high in fiber and protein include quinoa, brown rice, millet, and amaranth. Since they are naturally gluten-free, fruits and vegetables ought to be a mainstay of any gluten-free diet. Incorporating a range of complete foods not only makes it possible to have filling meals without worrying about gluten, but it also helps reduce the risk of nutrient shortages that are frequent in restricted diets. With a plethora of recipes showcasing their inherent flavors and textures, whole foods may add flavor and excitement to gluten-free eating.

Whole foods can be quite helpful in controlling symptoms and fostering general wellness, which is why people with chronic illnesses frequently turn to them for comfort. Whole foods are perfect for people trying to get healthier because they typically include fewer added sugars, bad fats, and preservatives. Whole grains, for instance, can promote digestive health, while anti-inflammatory foods like berries, leafy greens, and fatty fish can help reduce chronic inflammation. People can improve their quality of life by creating balanced meals that support their individual health demands by concentrating on nutrient-dense, whole foods.

In order to support the best possible health results, nutritionists and wellness experts recommend incorporating whole foods into different dietary frameworks. Whole foods' adaptability enables customized meal regimens that honor each person's needs and tastes. Clients might be encouraged to experiment with new ingredients and preparation techniques by being educated on the advantages of whole foods. Wellness practitioners can assist people in developing a closer relationship with their food by using whole foods as the basis for dietary recommendations. This can result in more conscious eating practices and long-lasting lifestyle adjustments.

Exploring whole foods and finding new flavors and textures that improve the dining experience can be enjoyable for culinary adventurers. Whole foods can be prepared in a variety of inventive ways, including as roasting, grilling, fermenting, and sprouting. Innovative recipes that highlight the inherent goodness of products and satisfy a range of dietary requirements may result from this investigation. In addition to providing nourishment, whole foods stimulate culinary creativity, enabling people to explore a journey of flavor and well-being. The combination of culinary art and health can result in energizing and healthful meals as the demand for whole foods keeps rising.

Handling Allergies to Food

For people who follow the whole foods diet, controlling food sensitivities is essential to leading a healthy lifestyle. A variety of negative reactions, from little discomfort to serious health issues, can be brought on by food allergies. Anyone hoping to survive on a diet high in natural, unadulterated foods must know how to recognize and treat these sensitivities. Through raising knowledge and implementing useful tactics, people can minimize the risks related to allergens while still reaping the advantages of complete foods.

Accurately identifying the particular allergens is the first step in controlling food allergies. This frequently entails recording any symptoms that appear after consuming particular meals in a thorough food journal. Dairy, wheat, peanuts, tree nuts, soy, eggs, fish, and shellfish are among the common allergies. Speaking with a medical expert or allergist can yield insightful information and may involve blood or skin testing to confirm allergies. After identifying the allergens, people can start to confidently manage their diets by avoiding potentially dangerous foods.

It doesn't have to be difficult to include entire foods in a diet that is sensitive to allergies. Whole foods, like fruits, vegetables, grains, and legumes, can be the cornerstone of a healthy, gratifying, and safe meal plan. Making food from home gives you more control over the materials and helps you stay away from allergens. Furthermore, employing substitute ingredients can enhance the culinary experience. For instance, using gluten-free grains like quinoa or brown rice in place of wheat-based items and substituting almond or coconut milk for dairy can both improve the culinary experience.

For food allergies to be effectively managed, education is essential. People should get familiar with food labels and learn how to spot hidden allergies. Numerous packaged goods may be prepared in facilities where cross-contamination happens or may include allergy residues. Making educated decisions can be facilitated by learning to identify words and components that may indicate possible allergies. Moreover, educating family members and friends can lower the chance of unintentional exposure by fostering a supportive environment where everyone is aware of dietary limitations.

Finally, for people dealing with food allergies, support systems and the community can be quite helpful. Participating in online networks or local groups can offer emotional support, recipe ideas, and resources. Exploring new whole food dishes that accommodate dietary restrictions can be a fulfilling way for foodies to learn about a variety of flavors and cooking methods. People can fully appreciate the journey of robust health that comes with a whole foods lifestyle by adopting a proactive approach to controlling food sensitivities.

Keeping Nutritional Needs in Balance

Achieving optimal health and well-being requires balancing nutritional demands, particularly for individuals following a whole foods diet. This method places a strong emphasis on eating natural, unprocessed foods that are free of the chemicals and preservatives included in many manufactured goods yet nevertheless contain vital nutrients. To maximize the advantages of a whole foods lifestyle and make sure that people get enough vitamins, minerals, and macronutrients for body functioning, it is essential to understand how to balance these nutritional components

Whole grains, legumes, nuts, seeds, fruits, and vegetables make up the majority of a whole foods diet. Every food group is essential for supplying particular nutrients. For instance, while beans provide protein and fiber, leafy greens are high in vitamins A, C, and K. Complex carbs, which are necessary for energy, are found in whole grains. People should try to include a range of these items in their daily meals in order to have a balanced diet. In addition to improving nutrient intake, this type supports a varied gut microbiota, which is associated with better digestion and general health.

Keeping Nutritional Needs in Balance

A whole foods diet must also carefully balance macronutrients, such as proteins, lipids, and carbohydrates. The body is fueled by carbohydrates from whole grains and fruits, and hormone production and cell structure are supported by healthy fats from nuts, seeds, and avocados. Protein-rich foods like quinoa, lentils, and beans are essential for immunological response and tissue repair. Maintaining energy levels, promoting appropriate body composition, and supporting satiety can all be achieved by finding the ideal balance between these macronutrients. Although keeping a meal journal might be helpful, it's crucial to pay attention to one's body and modify based on activity levels and individual needs.

Vitamins and minerals are examples of micronutrients that are equally crucial for attaining nutritional equilibrium. Although whole foods are naturally high in these micronutrients, people should be aware of their individual requirements, particularly if they have long-term medical issues or dietary limitations. For example, people on a plant-based diet might need to be more mindful of iron, omega-3 fatty acids, and vitamin B12. Since different colors frequently correspond to different nutrients, including a variety of colorful fruits and vegetables can help cover many micronutrient bases. Based on each person's unique health profile, dietary changes can also be guided by routine examinations with medical professionals.

Keeping Nutritional Needs in Balance

Last but not least, balancing nutritional demands involves more than simply dietary decisions; it also includes lifestyle choices including stress reduction, sleep patterns, and hydration. For the body to absorb nutrients and perform its general activities, enough hydration is essential. Furthermore, the regulation of hunger and metabolism can be greatly impacted by both enough sleep and efficient stress management. People can develop a holistic approach to health that supports mental and emotional resilience in addition to physical well-being by taking these aspects into account when following a whole foods diet. Adopting this holistic viewpoint enables experts and health enthusiasts to promote a healthy and sustainable way of living.

Finally, for people dealing with food allergies, support systems and the community can be quite helpful. Participating in online networks or local groups can offer emotional support, recipe ideas, and resources. Exploring new whole food dishes that accommodate dietary restrictions can be a fulfilling way for foodies to learn about a variety of flavors and cooking methods. People can fully appreciate the journey of robust health that comes with a whole foods lifestyle by adopting a proactive approach to controlling food sensitivities.

Whole Foods and Mental Wellness

THE ROLE OF NUTRITION IN MENTAL HEALTH

Because it affects mood and cognitive function, nutrition is crucial to mental health. The relationship between our nutrition and our emotions is becoming more and more evident in research, highlighting the significance of eating a diet abundant in nutrients. The building blocks for neurotransmitters, which are essential for brain transmission, are found in whole meals that are high in vitamins, minerals, and antioxidants. People can promote their mental health and lower their risk of mood disorders like anxiety and depression by making whole foods a priority.

One of the main areas of interest in comprehending the connection between diet and mental health is the gut-brain connection. Trillions of bacteria make up the gut microbiome, which is important for the synthesis of neurotransmitters including dopamine and serotonin. Better mental health outcomes are promoted by a diet rich in whole foods, such as fruits, vegetables, whole grains, and legumes, which also cultivate a healthy gut flora. Yogurt and kimchi are examples of fermented foods that further improve gut health since they include healthy microorganisms that have a favorable impact on mood and cognitive function.

Another important component that connects nutrition to mental health is inflammation. Anxiety and sadness are among the mental health conditions that have been linked to chronic inflammation. Whole foods include anti-inflammatory qualities that can help reduce this risk, especially those high in omega-3 fatty acids, antioxidants, and polyphenols. Foods that lower inflammation in the body, like leafy greens, berries, almonds, and fatty fish, can enhance mental and emotional well-being.

Additionally, micronutrients are crucial for preserving mental wellness. Mood disorders and cognitive decline have been associated with vitamin and mineral deficiencies, including those in B vitamins, vitamin D, zinc, and magnesium. Adequate consumption of these vital micronutrients can be ensured by following a whole foods diet, which places an emphasis on a range of nutrient-rich foods. People can improve their general well-being and support their mental health by including a wide variety of fruits, vegetables, whole grains, and lean meats in their diet.

Including whole foods in daily meals is a holistic approach to health that takes into account mental, emotional, and physical well-being; it is not only a dietary decision. Focusing on nutrient-dense, minimally processed foods can help people lay the groundwork for their best possible mental health. This dietary philosophy promotes awareness of how nutrition directly affects mood and cognitive function by encouraging mindfulness when making food choices. By embracing the power of nutrition, wellness experts, foodies, and health enthusiasts may encourage people to make dietary decisions that promote vibrant health and well-being.

FOODS TO IMPROVE CONCENTRATION AND MOOD

In addition to promoting physical health, nourishing the body with nutritious meals is important for improving mood and concentration. There is a well-established link between diet and mental health, with some foods providing particular advantages that can improve mood and focus. Whole foods, which are high in nutrients and less processed, may have a beneficial effect on brain chemistry by supplying the elements required for the best possible emotional stability and cognitive performance.

One of the most effective nutrients for improving mood is omega-3 fatty acids. These good fats, which are rich in fatty fish like salmon, sardines, and trout, are vital for brain function and have been connected to decreased rates of anxiety and sadness. Sources like as walnuts, chia seeds, and flaxseeds can offer a vegetarian substitute for people on a plant-based diet. By using these items in meals, a strong basis for increased emotional stability and mental clarity can be established.

Fruits and vegetables high in antioxidants are also essential for improving mood and concentration. Vitamins, minerals, and phytochemicals found in foods like sweet potatoes, spinach, and blueberries help the brain fight off oxidative stress. Eating a diverse range of produce can help safeguard and improve the brain's function because stress can cause mood problems and cognitive loss. A diet high in these colorful foods promotes mental clarity and a more optimistic attitude in addition to physical health.

Yogurt, kefir, sauerkraut, kimchi, and other fermented foods are vital for gut health, which is increasingly linked to mental health. The gut-brain axis emphasizes how mood management and digestive health are related. Fermented foods contain probiotics that can help maintain a healthy gut microbiota, which can affect brain chemistry and lessen depressive and anxious feelings. By incorporating these foods into a whole foods diet, one can promote a healthy gut-brain link that improves mental and emotional well-being in general.

Lastly, complex carbohydrates, which are essential for long-lasting energy and concentration, are found in whole grains and legumes. Quinoa, brown rice, lentils, and chickpeas are among the foods that release glucose into the bloodstream gradually, avoiding energy crashes that can impair mood and focus. In addition to being rich in nutrients, these foods are also high in fiber, which promotes healthy digestion and helps keep blood sugar levels steady. People can enhance their emotional and cognitive health and lead more balanced, lively lives by giving whole grains and legumes priority in their diet.

Techniques for Mindful Eating

Conscious awareness of the food we eat and the eating experience itself are key components of mindful eating practices. By encouraging people to participate completely in their meals, this method promotes healthier choices and a stronger bond with food. People can develop an appreciation for complete foods and their nutritional advantages by slowing down and focusing on the sensory elements of eating, such as taste, texture, and scent. In addition to improving the dining experience, this method facilitates digestion and helps avoid overindulging.

The significance of setting up a comfortable dining space is a fundamental component of mindful eating. This entails reducing distractions during meals, such as screens, loud noises, and multitasking. People can concentrate on their food in a relaxed and welcoming environment, which makes it simpler to identify signs of hunger and fullness. By allocating specific time for meals, one may encourage a more deliberate approach to food selection and turn eating from a rushed necessity into a joyful ritual.

The advantages of mindful eating can be increased by including entire foods in your routine. Whole foods include a multitude of nutrients that promote general health because they are lightly processed and devoid of additives. People can enjoy the natural flavors of fresh fruits, vegetables, entire grains, lean meats, and healthy fats while simultaneously nourishing their bodies. This promotes a deeper understanding of the variety and depth of whole foods, inspiring people to experiment with novel cooking techniques and recipes that support their health objectives.

Self-reflection is another essential element of mindful eating. People can have a better awareness of where their food comes from and how it affects both their health and the environment by taking the time to think about where their food originates from. This activity can increase awareness of individual food choices and cultivate appreciation for the work of farmers and producers. By keeping a journal of their meals, emotions, and experiences, people can also spot trends in their eating behaviors and make more thoughtful choices going forward.

Lastly, people who are managing long-term medical issues may find that mindful eating techniques are an effective aid. Being present at meals can assist people who are managing dietary restrictions or who want to maximize their nutrition in determining which foods promote their well-being and which do not. A more intuitive approach to eating may result from this increased awareness, allowing for more flexibility and enjoyment without sacrificing health. People can have a more balanced connection with food and enhance their health and quality of life by including mindful eating into their daily routines.

Chapter 8
Whole Foods for Families

Introducing Whole Foods to Children

One of the most important steps in fostering lifetime good eating habits in children is exposing them to whole foods. Fruits, vegetables, whole grains, nuts, seeds, and legumes are examples of whole foods that offer vital nutrients without the processing and additives frequently found in packaged foods. Parents and other adults who care for children can empower them to make dietary decisions that support their general health by introducing them to these nutrient-dense foods. The intention is to foster a culture that not only embraces but also celebrates whole meals.

Using hands-on activities to introduce whole meals to kids is a good strategy. Their interest and curiosity about food might be piqued by involving children in meal preparation. Children feel more in control of their meals when they help wash veggies, combine ingredients, or even choose what to buy at the grocery store. This interaction helps them have a better awareness of the origins of their food and emphasizes the value of selecting fresh, unadulterated foods. Additionally, cooking together can develop into a treasured family pastime, promoting the notion that eating healthily is a fun and social activity.

Promoting whole foods in youngsters can also be greatly aided by educational programs. Children can learn about the advantages of eating a whole foods diet through nutrition education programs in schools and the community. Nutrition education may be made engaging through interactive courses that include sampling sessions, cooking demonstrations, and interesting facts about fruits and vegetables. Children are more likely to accept the concept of whole foods as a regular component of their diet if a nurturing atmosphere that promotes inquiry and discovery is established.

Furthermore, knowing children's aversions and preferences is necessary when introducing them to entire meals. To help children discover flavors they like, it is crucial to be persistent and patient while providing a range of complete food options. Reducing resistance can be achieved by gradually adding these foods to their meals. For example, adding diced veggies to spaghetti or incorporating spinach into a fruit smoothie can bring fresh flavors without overpowering them. Children may adjust and learn to value full foods without feeling rushed thanks to this steady approach.

Last but not least, promoting the value of whole foods requires setting an example of healthy eating habits. Since kids tend to imitate their parents' and other caregivers' behaviors, fostering a healthy connection with food can have a long-lasting effect. You set a strong example by emphasizing whole foods in your personal diet and sharing your passion for wholesome meals. Honoring the rich hues and varied textures of whole meals can encourage kids to try and love these choices as well, which will ultimately result in a healthier future for coming generations.

Ideas for Family Meals

Family meals are crucial for fostering relationships and good health. Families can enjoy wholesome meals that promote fitness and a feeling of community by emphasizing whole food items. Whole food preparation promotes the use of fresh, unprocessed foodstuffs that minimize additives and preservatives while providing vital nutrients. Families can use this method to provide delectable, filling meals that fit a range of dietary requirements and taste preferences.

A vibrant stir-fried vegetable dish over quinoa or brown rice is a great idea for a family dinner. In addition to adding nutritious value, including seasonal veggies like bell peppers, broccoli, and carrots makes the dish look nice. Lean protein foods, such as shrimp, chicken, or tofu, can improve the meal's satiety. Flavor can be added without using processed condiments by using whole food-based sauces, like homemade ginger-garlic sauce or tamari. This dish is easy to make and may be tailored to the tastes of the family.

A filling bean and vegetable chili is another healthy family dinner option. A nutrient-dense, high-protein, high-fiber dish can be made with dried beans, tomatoes, and a variety of veggies like kale, sweet potatoes, and zucchini. To create a strong taste profile, add fresh herbs, chili powder, and cumin. Because it can be prepared in bulk, this dish is ideal for freezing for later use or for leftovers. It offers texture and extra nutrients when served over brown rice or with healthy grain toast.

Ideas for Family Meals

Family meals are crucial for fostering relationships and good health. Families can enjoy wholesome meals that promote fitness and a feeling of community by emphasizing whole food items. Whole food preparation promotes the use of fresh, unprocessed foodstuffs that minimize additives and preservatives while providing vital nutrients. Families can use this method to provide delectable, filling meals that fit a range of dietary requirements and taste preferences.

A vibrant stir-fried vegetable dish over quinoa or brown rice is a great idea for a family dinner. In addition to adding nutritious value, including seasonal veggies like bell peppers, broccoli, and carrots makes the dish look nice. Lean protein foods, such as shrimp, chicken, or tofu, can improve the meal's satiety. Flavor can be added without using processed condiments by using whole food-based sauces, like homemade ginger-garlic sauce or tamari. This dish is easy to make and may be tailored to the tastes of the family.

A filling bean and vegetable chili is another healthy family dinner option. A nutrient-dense, high-protein, high-fiber dish can be made with dried beans, tomatoes, and a variety of veggies like kale, sweet potatoes, and zucchini. To create a strong taste profile, add fresh herbs, chili powder, and cumin. Because it can be prepared in bulk, this dish is ideal for freezing for later use or for leftovers. It offers texture and extra nutrients when served over brown rice or with healthy grain toast.

A salad bar that focuses on healthy foods is a healthier choice. Arrange a range of toppings, such as roasted vegetables, leafy greens, nuts, seeds, and a variety of dressings made with whole foods like vinegar, olive oil, and fresh herbs. This arrangement enables kids to try different flavors and textures while also letting family members personalize their salads to suit their preferences. This dish can be made more substantial while remaining light and refreshing by include a protein source such hard-boiled eggs, chickpeas, or grilled chicken.

Lastly, a healthy and enjoyable family supper suggestion is to have a breakfast that is inspired by whole foods for dinner. A tasty, wholesome, and warming supper can include whole grain pancakes or oats topped with yogurt, fresh fruit, and almonds. While providing a filling choice, adding veggies to omelets or frittatas can improve their nutritional profile. Because everyone may help prepare the meals, this method not only breaks up the routine of conventional dinners but also encourages inventive cooking and family time.

Promoting Nutritious Eating Practices

Promoting wholesome eating practices is crucial for anybody pursuing vibrant health, particularly for those experimenting with the whole foods diet. This method places a strong emphasis on eating natural, unadulterated foods that are high in nutrients and devoid of artificial additives. People can better nourish their bodies, improve their well-being, and develop a sustainable lifestyle by emphasizing whole foods. Creating a setting that encourages healthy choices is the first step in accomplishing this. This can involve reducing the amount of processed food and sugary drinks in kitchens while increasing the amount of fresh fruits, vegetables, whole grains, nuts, and seeds.

In order to promote good eating habits, education is essential. People should try to learn about the nutritional worth of different foods and how they affect general health, especially health lovers and food adventurers. Workshops, cooking lessons, and educational materials can improve understanding of food preparation methods, meal planning, and the advantages of eating seasonally. People can make better decisions that support their objectives if they are given a broader understanding of the sources of food and how nutrition affects health.

Mindful eating, which is being present and paying attention to the eating experience, is another crucial component. People are encouraged by this method to enjoy every bite, identify signs of hunger and fullness, and value the tastes and textures of whole foods. Reducing overeating and fostering a more fulfilling relationship with food are two benefits of mindful eating. It can also make meals more enjoyable, turning eating from a rushed task into a joyful activity that promotes relationships with others and with oneself.

Maintaining long-term healthy eating habits requires incorporating variety into the diet. Promoting culinary exploration can encourage people to experiment with various whole food items and attempt new recipes. This guarantees a varied nutrient intake in addition to keeping meals interesting. People can experience flavors and sensations they may not have previously thought of by introducing them to new fruits, vegetables, and grains, turning eating healthily into an enjoyable journey rather than a work.

Lastly, motivation and responsibility can be greatly increased by establishing reasonable goals and monitoring progress. People can benefit from using applications that encourage healthy eating or from keeping a food log. A community of like-minded people can offer support and encouragement by hearing about experiences, which can lessen the intimidating nature of the path to robust health. People can develop long-lasting healthy eating habits that support the whole foods diet's tenets and eventually enhance their health and well-being by acknowledging and appreciating their little triumphs and keeping an optimistic outlook.

Chapter 9
Overcoming Challenges

Common Obstacles and Solutions

People frequently run across common problems when they start eating a whole foods diet. The availability of whole foods in some places is one of the main obstacles. Many people reside in areas known as "food deserts," where there are few options for nutritious foods and fresh produce. It may become challenging to stick with the lifestyle as a result of dissatisfaction and a sense of defeat. Health aficionados can take steps to remedy this issue by looking for local farmers' markets, participating in community-supported agriculture initiatives, or investigating whole food-focused online grocery delivery services. Furthermore, supporting neighborhood projects that increase food access can aid in laying the groundwork for long-lasting community transformation.

The misconception about entire meals and how to prepare them is another major obstacle. Many people think that using entire products in cooking calls for a high level of culinary expertise or a significant time investment. Even the most passionate people may be discouraged from embracing the whole foods diet due to this misperception. Nutritionists and wellness experts can counter this by providing workshops or online courses that demythologize cooking. Quick, easy recipes that emphasize the convenience and adaptability of whole foods can encourage people to try new things in the kitchen without feeling overburdened. Culinary adventurers can develop a sense of camaraderie by exchanging cooking advice via online platforms.

Adopting a whole foods diet is frequently influenced by financial limitations. Whole foods might occasionally seem more costly than processed substitutes, which makes many wonder if adopting this lifestyle is really feasible. But it's important to understand that spending money on healthy foods can result in long-term savings on chronic illness-related medical expenses. People might favor seasonal food, which is typically more flavorful and less expensive, to lessen the financial load. Buying grains, legumes, and nuts in bulk might also be a smart move. Professionals in nutrition can help people plan meals that avoid waste and budget for nutritious foods.

Another typical challenge for people making the switch to a whole foods diet is time management. Making meals from scratch might be difficult for people with busy schedules, so many turn to convenience foods. People can use batch cooking techniques and meal planning to get beyond this obstacle. Time can be saved during busy weekdays by allocating a few hours each week to dinner preparation. Cooking may be made even easier by promoting the use of quick pots and slow cookers. Within groups of health enthusiasts, exchanging quick recipes and meal prep ideas can encourage accountability and drive.

Finally, people may find it difficult to fully commit to a whole foods lifestyle due to emotional and psychological obstacles. It might be challenging for many people to alter their eating habits because they have strong emotional attachments to particular processed foods. Mindfulness exercises that promote a healthy relationship with eating can help people deal with this. Online forums or support groups can offer a secure setting for discussing setbacks and victories, creating a feeling of community. By providing advice on emotional eating and assisting people in creating healthy coping mechanisms, nutritionists and wellness specialists can play a critical role. People can develop a more satisfying and long-lasting whole foods journey by tackling these emotional obstacles.

Maintaining Your Motivation While Traveling

Maintaining motivation on your path to robust health, particularly while following a whole foods diet, calls for a combination of personal dedication, community support, and information. Adopting whole foods frequently requires major lifestyle adjustments, which can be difficult. Gaining knowledge about the advantages of whole foods, such as increased vitality, elevated mood, and decreased risk of chronic illnesses, can be a strong incentive. Maintaining your dietary commitments is made simpler when you understand the real effects that nutrition has on your general health.

Setting attainable, unambiguous goals is crucial to sustaining motivation. These objectives must to be clear, quantifiable, and customized for your unique situation. For example, instead of just trying to eat healthier, think about making it a goal to cook a whole foods recipe twice a week or to include a different vegetable in your meals every week. You may maintain your interest in your quest and feel a feeling of accomplishment by taking these small measures. Whether you use a diary or a smartphone app, keeping track of your accomplishments will help you stay motivated and show off your improvement.

Support from the community is also essential for maintaining motivation. Whether through courses, local events, or online forums, surrounding yourself with like-minded people can offer accountability and support. You can improve your trip by developing a sense of camaraderie with others by sharing difficulties, recipes, and experiences. Participating in a community also creates learning and development possibilities since you can learn from others who are on similar journeys to wellness and health.

Adding diversity to your cooking and meals can also help you stay motivated. There are many different flavors, textures, and colors to choose from when following a whole foods diet, so it doesn't have to be boring. You can rekindle your love of cooking and eating well by experimenting with various cuisines or seasonal items. Eating healthily may be made more pleasurable by converting your kitchen into an exciting place for culinary exploration through cooking lessons or experimenting with new recipes.

Finally, it's critical to realize that setbacks are a normal part of any journey and to exercise self-compassion. Due to a hectic schedule, you might occasionally neglect meal preparation or overindulge in processed meals. Reframe these instances as teaching opportunities rather than failures. Evaluate the cause of the departure and how you might modify your strategy going forward. You will be better able to sustain your motivation and stick to your commitment to whole foods and robust health if you develop a mindset that values adaptability and growth.

Creating a Network of Support

Anyone starting a path toward vibrant health with the whole foods diet must establish a support system. This network can offer encouragement, responsibility, and useful tools that improve the process of changing to a healthy way of living. Being with like-minded people can have a big impact on your success, whether you are a nutrition and wellness expert, a person with chronic health difficulties, or just a foodie. There are many different types of support networks, such as online communities, local groups, friends, and family.

Building a support system frequently begins with interacting with friends and family. Talking about your objectives and plans with people you care about can help them understand and support you. Informing your loved ones on the advantages of whole meals can encourage them to follow your path or at the very least create a more encouraging atmosphere at home. Organizing dinners that highlight delectable whole food recipes can also spark their curiosity and demonstrate that flavor is not sacrificed for health.

Health and nutrition-focused local community organizations can offer a priceless network of support. These organizations frequently host cooking courses, workshops, and group activities that support whole foods. You can meet others who are as passionate about health and wellbeing as you are by taking part in these activities. These local ties can also result in collaborations for meal preparation, recipe sharing, and even fitness regimens, fostering a team-oriented environment that motivates everyone to maintain their objectives.

The process of creating support networks has been completely transformed by online communities. People can ask questions, seek advice, and share experiences in a variety of settings provided by social media platforms, forums, and specialized websites. For people who might not have access to local support groups or who feel more at ease discussing their journeys online, these virtual networks can be especially helpful. By participating in these groups, materials like meal plans, recipes, and advice on how to overcome obstacles associated with the whole foods diet can be shared.

Last but not least, as a health enthusiast, think about helping others. By sharing your personal insights and experiences, you can inspire others to lead healthier lives. Through social media, blogging, or neighborhood gatherings, your story can motivate others and create a sense of community among those working toward comparable health objectives. In addition to improving your own health journey, developing and maintaining a support system helps others and fosters a healthy community centered around whole foods and robust health.

CHAPTER 10
Celebrating Your Progress

Reflecting on Your Journey

One crucial technique to improve your comprehension of the life-changing potential of whole foods is to reflect on your experience. It is crucial to pause and reflect on your beginnings, your progress, and your accomplishments as you are fully embracing the whole foods diet. By engaging in this reflective activity, you can identify patterns and habits that may still require attention while also reaffirming your commitment to leading a healthier lifestyle. You may determine what has gone well, what obstacles you faced, and how you can keep improving on your journey to vibrant health by reviewing your progress.

Understanding how whole foods have affected your physical health is one of the most important parts of your journey. Many people find that switching from processed foods to a more natural, whole foods-based diet significantly improves their energy levels, digestion, and general well-being. Give these alterations in your body some thought. Do you have more energy now? Have you observed changes in your mood, sleep patterns, or skin? By reminding you of the advantages of your food decisions and motivating you to keep up these healthful practices, writing down these experiences can be a very effective motivator.

It's also crucial to consider the psychological and emotional facets of your journey. Your mental well-being and self-perception can be significantly impacted by the relationship you develop with food. Think about how changing to a whole foods diet has changed your perspective. Have you come to see food more positively, seeing it as nourishing for your body and soul as well as a source of sustenance? Eating with awareness can improve your overall food enjoyment and make your culinary adventures more rewarding.

This kind of interaction with food cultivates appreciation and thankfulness for the sustenance it offers.

Your path to thriving health also heavily depends on your social relationships. Consider how your eating habits have affected your interactions with friends and family. Have you encouraged people to try whole foods? Maybe you have found new networks or groups of people who share your enthusiasm for fitness and nutrition. Participating in cooking classes or seminars, exchanging recipes, and having conversations with others about food may all improve your experience and strengthen your dedication to a whole foods diet. These relationships foster a feeling of purpose in pursuing health and wellness in addition to offering support.

Finally, you must recognize that your journey is a continuous one. Wellness and health are dynamic; they necessitate ongoing education and adjustment. Thinking back on your trip can help you identify areas where you might wish to concentrate your future efforts. Every action you take, whether it's trying out new foods, improving your cooking methods, or learning more about nutrition, adds to a bigger story that affects your general health. Accept the notion that this is a lifetime endeavor that is enhanced by your encounters, realizations, and the relationships you form.

Telling Others About Your Experience

Talking to others about your experience can have a profound impact on your path to healthy health. As wellness and nutrition experts, chronic illness patients, foodies, and health enthusiasts, your perspectives can uplift and empower others around you. In addition to fortifying community relationships, this knowledge and experience sharing promotes a shared comprehension of the advantages of a whole foods diet. You may demystify the process for those who might be reluctant or uncertain about making comparable changes in their own lives by sharing your journey.

It's important to emphasize the precise dietary and lifestyle adjustments you made while talking about your experiences. Describe the many kinds of whole foods you included, including fruits, vegetables, whole grains, nuts, and seeds, and the effects they have had on your general health. People who are going through similar things might relate to personal stories regarding difficulties encountered, such switching from processed to natural foods or conquering cravings. This genuineness might inspire others to go out on their own adventures with more assurance by crafting a relevant story.

Sharing real-world advice and tactics can be just as beneficial as sharing personal tales. Talk about your grocery shopping, meal planning, and handling of potentially food-related social situations. For those wishing to follow a similar lifestyle, offering resources like preferred recipes, meal prep methods, or even a list of suggested whole food products can be a helpful guide. Talking about how whole foods affect mood, energy levels, and general health can encourage others to investigate these dietary adjustments.

Additionally, think about using a variety of platforms to reach more people. Sharing your journey through blogs, social media, or community workshops can be a great idea. Every platform has distinct chances to establish connections with various demographic groups that could profit from your perspectives. Working together with other wellness professionals can help you spread your message and build a strong support system. You may encourage more people to think about the benefits of a whole foods diet by sharing your experience in a variety of ways.

Finally, promote candid communication and community involvement. Create an environment where people feel at ease talking about their experiences with whole foods by inviting others to share their stories and queries. A sense of support and belonging are fostered by this interaction, which is crucial for any health journey. By discussing hardships, encouraging one another, and celebrating victories, we can build a strong group momentum that will benefit everyone's health. You may improve your own journey and support the flourishing health of your community by sharing your story.

Maintaining the Whole Foods Way of Life

Maintaining the Whole Foods Lifestyle entails embracing a comprehensive approach to wellness that incorporates mindfulness, exercise, and nutrition rather than merely following a diet. Understanding the fundamentals of whole foods is crucial for people with chronic illnesses and health enthusiasts to preserve their vigor and reach their long-term health objectives. Whole foods offer vital nutrients that support body functions and foster optimal health because they are minimally processed and devoid of artificial substances. People can improve their health and lower their chance of developing chronic illnesses by concentrating on these foods.

It is essential to develop behaviors that give priority to locally sourced, seasonal, and fresh foodstuffs if you want to successfully maintain a whole foods lifestyle. This could entail building a rapport with nearby producers or making frequent trips to farmers' markets. By teaching their customers the advantages of seasonal eating and how to include a range of fruits, vegetables, whole grains, nuts, and seeds in their meals, nutritionists and wellness specialists can play a crucial role. Stressing the value of variety in the diet not only improves nutritional intake but also keeps meals interesting and fulfilling, both of which are essential for sustained adherence to this eating pattern.

Maintaining a whole foods lifestyle requires careful meal planning and preparation. To make whole meals tasty and pleasurable, culinary explorers might try out various cooking methods and taste combinations. Preparing meals in advance lessens the temptation to rely on convenience, processed foods, which might compromise health objectives. Involving family members in the cooking process also promotes a feeling of belonging and a shared dedication to eating healthily. Another way to break up monotony and promote creativity in the kitchen is to create a rotating menu of whole food recipes.

Maintaining the whole foods lifestyle involves practicing mindfulness. People who engage in mindful eating are inspired to value the nutrients, flavors, and textures that entire meals offer. By lowering emotional eating and encouraging improved digestion, this method aids in the development of a more positive relationship with food. Integrating mindfulness exercises like yoga or meditation, which improve mental clarity and promote physical wellness, can be advantageous for health enthusiasts. Beyond the plate, mindful living encourages people to consider their entire lifestyle choices, such as stress reduction and physical activity.

Lastly, it's critical to maintain relationships with a group of people who share your commitment to holistic wellness and natural foods. Participating in workshops, local organizations, or internet forums can offer accountability, motivation, and support. People might be inspired to keep going on their path to vibrant health by sharing their experiences, struggles, and victories. The whole foods lifestyle's tenets are reinforced by creating a network of support, which makes it simpler to overcome obstacles and recognize progress along the way. People may make sure that their dedication to whole foods becomes a significant aspect of their lives by building relationships and never stopping learning.

Printed in Great Britain
by Amazon